D1163758

ZACK RYDER

BY JASON BRICKWEG

WOO WOO WOO

RYDER

TORQUE ™

BELLWETHER MEDIA · MINNEAPOLIS, MN

Are you ready to take it to the extreme?
Torque books thrust you into the action-packed world
of sports, vehicles, mystery, and adventure. These books
may include dirt, smoke, fire, and dangerous stunts.
WARNING : read at your own risk.

Library of Congress Cataloging-in-Publication Data

Brickweg, Jason.
 Zack Ryder / by Jason Brickweg.
   p. cm. -- (Torque: Pro wrestling champions)
 Includes bibliographical references and index.
 Summary: "Engaging images accompany information about Zack Ryder. The combination of high-interest subject matter and light text is intended for students in grades 3 through 7"--Provided by publisher.
 ISBN 978-1-60014-905-4 (hardcover : alk. paper)
 1. Ryder, Zack, 1985---Juvenile literature. 2. Wrestlers--United States--Biography--Juvenile literature. I. Title.
 GV1196.R94B75 2013
 796.812092--dc23
 [B]   2012041216

This edition first published in 2013 by Bellwether Media, Inc.

Printed in the United States of America, North Mankato, MN.

The images in this book are reproduced through the courtesy of: Devin Chen, front cover, pp. 9-10, 18-19, 20-21; Getty Images, pp. 4, 6, 14-15, 16-17; Zuma Press/Newscom, pp. 4-5, 12-13; Sebastian Kahnert/

CONTENTS

WARNING!

The wrestling moves used in this book are performed
by professionals. Do not attempt to reenact any
of the moves performed in this book.

UNITED STATES CHAMPION

World Wrestling Entertainment (WWE) fans roared for Zack Ryder. They wanted him to defeat Dolph Ziggler at the 2011 Tables, Ladders, and Chairs event. Ziggler had control of the match. Then Ryder delivered a **dropkick**, a **clothesline**, and the **Broski Boot**. Ziggler was down.

DOLPH ZIGGLER

Wrestling Name:	Zack Ryder
Real Name:	Matt Cardona
Height:	6 feet, 2 inches (1.9 meters)
Weight:	214 pounds (97 kilograms)
Started Wrestling:	2004
Finishing Move:	Rough Ryder

Suddenly Ziggler's manager interfered to stop the count. Ziggler was on his feet again. The two battled back and forth. Then Ryder did a **Hurricanrana** from the top rope. Soon he finished Ziggler off with the Rough Ryder. After three counts, Ryder was the United States Champion!

ZACK RYDER?

Zack Ryder's real name is Matt Cardona. He was born on May 14, 1985 in Merrick, New York. Cardona spent a lot of time at the local comic book store growing up. He loved reading about Wolverine and other action heroes.

Cardona eventually decided he wanted to become an action hero. He started wrestling in the **independent circuit**. In 2004, he **debuted** in the New York Wrestling Connection as Brett Matthews. He and Brian Myers formed a **tag team**.

CARDONA

MYERS

QUICK HIT!

Cardona and Myers called
themselves The Majors Brothers.

In 2006, Cardona and Myers each
signed a **developmental contract** with
WWE. They wrestled in Deep South
Wrestling and Ohio Valley Wrestling.
They won tag team championships in
both of these smaller leagues.

BECOMING A CHAMPION

Cardona entered WWE's main ring in 2007. He continued to wrestle with Myers. That year, the pair dressed like Edge to help him win the World Heavyweight Championship. They became **heels**. Soon their ring names changed. Cardona became Zack Ryder and Myers became Curt Hawkins. Ryder and Hawkins won the Tag Team Championship in 2008.

QUICK HIT!

Ryder and Hawkins were the youngest wrestlers to win the Tag Team Championship.

Ryder began wrestling on his own in 2009. He transformed into the Long Island Loudmouth. Suddenly he had short hair, tan skin, and a cocky attitude. In 2011, he beat Dolph Ziggler to claim his first singles title. The tag team champion became an individual champion!

QUICK HIT!

Ryder posted videos on the Internet to attract fans. It worked. In 2011, he called himself the Internet Champion.

MISSILE
DROPKICK

Opponents expect certain moves from Ryder. The Missile Dropkick is one **signature move**. He jumps from the top rope and kicks the opponent with both feet. Ryder also uses the Zack Attack. He brings the opponent's neck to his shin and then flips him over.

ROUGH
RYDER

Ryder likes to end matches with the Rough Ryder. This **finishing move** comes before a pin. Ryder runs toward his opponent. Then he jumps and wraps his legs around the opponent's head to knock him down. The Rough Ryder keeps Zack Ryder on top of his game!

GLOSSARY

Broski Boot—a move in which Zack Ryder charges and takes his boot to an opponent sitting in the corner

Clothesline—a move in which a wrestler slams a charging opponent with his outstretched arm

debuted—first appeared

developmental contract—an agreement in which a wrestler signs with WWE but then wrestles in smaller leagues to gain experience and develop skills

dropkick—a move in which a wrestler jumps and then kicks an opponent with both feet

finishing move—a wrestling move meant to finish off an opponent so that he can be pinned

heels—wrestlers seen by fans as villains

Hurricanrana—a move in which a wrestler locks his legs around an opponent's neck and then flips backward to pull the opponent to the ground

independent circuit—the minor league of professional wrestling

signature move—a move that a wrestler is famous for performing

tag team—two wrestlers who compete as a team

TO LEARN MORE

AT THE LIBRARY

Black, Jake. *The Ultimate Guide to WWE*. New York, N.Y.: Grosset & Dunlap, 2011.

Gordon, Nick. *Dolph Ziggler*. Minneapolis, Minn.: Bellwether Media, Inc., 2012.

Price, Sean Stewart. *The Kids' Guide to Pro Wrestling*. Mankato, Minn.: Edge Books, 2012.

ON THE WEB

Learning more about Zack Ryder is as easy as 1, 2, 3.

1. Go to www.factsurfer.com.

2. Enter "Zack Ryder" into the search box.

3. Click the "Surf" button and you will see a list of related Web sites.

With factsurfer.com, finding more information is just a click away.

INDEX